Tra... an Empath Uncovered

Discover Who You Are and Why You're Here

By

Diane Kathrine

Copyright ©2017 Diane Kathrine

All rights reserved. This book or any portion thereof may not be reproduced or used in any manner whatsoever without the express written permission of the author, except for the use of brief quotations in articles or book reviews.

The author of this book does not dispense medical advice or prescribe the use of any technique as a form of treatment for physical or medical problems without the advice of a physician or specialist, either directly or indirectly. The author's intent is to offer information of a general nature to help you in your quest to find complete balance. Should you use any of the information in this book for yourself, the author assumes no responsibility for your actions. If professional advice or other expert assistance is required, the services of a competent professional should be sought.

Contents

Trait 1: The Knowing — 1

Trait 2: Being in Public Places is Overwhelming — 5

Trait 3: Feeling Others' Emotions and Taking Them on as Their Own — 13

Trait 4: Watching Violence, Cruelty or Tragedy on TV is Unbearable — 23

Trait 5: An Empath can Feel a Lie — 27

Trait 6: Experiences Physical Symptoms of Another — 33

Trait 7: Suffers Digestive Disorders and Lower Back Problems — 39

Trait 8: Looks Out for the Underdog — 43

Trait 9: Friends & Strangers Offload Their Problems — 49

Trait 10: Often Endures Chronic Empath Fatigue — 53

Trait 11: Owns an Addictive Personality — 57

Trait 12: Drawn to the Metaphysical and Healing Therapies — 63

Trait 13:	Enjoys Being Creative	67
Trait 14:	Love of Nature and Animals	73
Trait 15:	Need for Solitude	77
Trait 16:	Gets Bored or Distracted Easily	81
Trait 17:	Finds It Impossible to Do What They Do Not Enjoy	85
Trait 18:	Strives for the Truth	89
Trait 19:	Always Looking for Answers	95
Trait 20:	Craves Adventure, Freedom and Travel	99
Trait 21:	Abhors Clutter	103
Trait 22:	Loves to Daydream and Overthink	107
Trait 23:	Finds Routine, Rules or Control Imprisoning	111
Trait 24:	Prone to Carry Weight Without Overeating	117
Trait 25:	Excellent Listener	121

Trait 26: Intolerance to Narcissism 127

Trait 27: The Ability to Feel the Days of the Week 131

Trait 28: Will Not Choose to Buy Antiques, Vintage or Second-Hand 133

Trait 29: Senses the Energy of Food 137

Trait 30: Can Appear Moody, Shy, Aloof or Disconnected 141

Introduction

Misunderstood traits are a major cause of unhappiness within the Empath. Not being able to talk openly about their traits, or how they make them feel, can lead to a sense of isolation and an inability to connect with others.

Modern life poses challenges for every human, but for the Empath these challenges are heightened because they sense everything so intensely. Even from a young age, Empaths know they are different, although they are mostly unaware of the reason for this. Empaths possess many extraordinary traits and boast an incredibly rare emotional intelligence; but they can also be unsure how to capitalize on these gifts. This lack of understanding may hold them back from walking their destined or desired path.

If they don't know who they are, why they are different or understand their ways, the unknowing Empath faces an awkward existence. But it does not have to be that way.

I have been writing about ways to help Empaths since early 2011. It was after realizing there was very little information available on the subject that I decided to share what I knew, and had discovered, on my blog. One of my first posts being: '*30 Traits of an Empath*'. Nearly six years later and that list of traits has been shared hundreds of thousands of times, in one way or another, and has helped many identify themselves as an Empath.

This book takes a deeper look into those same Empath traits, and offers a broader explanation into their meaning, the effect they have on everyday life, and presents ways to overcome any difficulties they may pose. I hope it also offers comfort in the knowing that these seemingly 'peculiar traits' are shared by many and are just a normal part of Empath life.

Life as an Empath is not an easy path to walk, I know, but when we identify our traits, and grasp the meaning behind them, life makes more sense.

We all deserve happiness and joy, and there is no reason why we should not be living this way. It may not seem so now—especially if you often suffer with overwhelm, Sensitivity stress or fatigue—but a blissful life is completely attainable when we understand our traits, gain mastery over them, and find balance.

For the Empath, the right knowledge is power! Knowing, understanding and accepting the traits of an Empath presents the keys to emotional freedom and happiness... we just need to unlock the doors.

This book is a journey into a better understanding of Empath truths. By the time you have finished reading, you will have gained a greater understanding of your Empath traits and know how to work with them to get the very best out of life.

Not only will this book help you understand why you feel everything so powerfully, why you suffer intense bouts of fatigue and emotional overload, but it also takes a look at quick-fix ways to help you get through social situations, increase your energy and feel better about yourself.

You have already signed up to life as an Empath. You signed up because you were ready to experience the path of a 'Sensitive' and the pleasure and pain that comes with it.

An Empath's life is never dull. At times, it will be filled with absolute joy and happiness or it may prove to be a tempestuous, steep and jagged climb. Whatever your journey presents the rewards of scaling such highs and lows become more evident with each passing year. So much so, you become grateful for having been given such a rare opportunity to experience everything so powerfully.

So, without any further ado, let's uncover and review: the traits of an Empath, written just for you!

Trait 1

The Knowing

Empaths just know stuff. It is a Knowing that goes way beyond intuition or simple gut-feelings; even though that is how many would describe the "Knowing". The more attuned the Empath, the stronger this gift becomes.

Intuition comes in many forms: foreseeing future events, being psychic, or having the ability to read others, etc. For most Empaths, however, their intuition simply comes as a powerful awareness.

The part of the brain responsible for intuition is heightened within the Empath (along with the part for empathy) and this is why they have such a strong sense of Knowing.

They are born into their intuitive nature and the more they tune into it, the more potent it becomes. By finding balance, and with patience and practice, their intuition can be significantly developed to the point it is a trusted source of guidance.

Every Empath has intuition to varying degrees. For most, it will be felt as strong stirrings within the gut area in regard to certain stimuli. For example: when we first meet someone, we may get a tremendous sense of dread, in the gut, and a notion that this person is bad news. (The stronger the feeling, the starker the warning.) We may then, however, convince ourselves that our suspicions are silly and speculative, and dismiss these strong gut-stirrings. Quickly putting them to the back of our mind. In many cases, these ignored warnings come back to haunt us, when said person causes us, or a loved one, trouble or pain.

Here's another example of how our intuition works to protect us: On a visit to a bank we are advised, by the manager, where to invest our money for the greatest return. On hearing the recommendations, we experience a gut-burning dread within the solar-plexus. We ignore this sensation, whilst telling ourselves the bank manager would not advise us to invest if it was not the soundest idea (I think you know where this is heading). Months or years down the line, we discover those investments were indeed a bad idea, and we lost money instead of increasing it.

We disregard our gut-feelings (Knowing) for many reasons. Perhaps we want to see the best in others or maybe we do not completely believe in our intuitive nature. There is also the possibility that if our intuition is guiding us in a direction which does not fit in with our plans, or desires, we will choose to ignore it. But these gut-feelings are there to warn, serve and protect us from experiencing unnecessary pain (We already take on enough as it is).

Overwhelming gut-sensations are powerful indicators of when something is amiss and should never be rejected or ignored. This strong sense of Knowing is unique to each of us and is our guide and wayshower. It helps us discern between right or wrong life-choices, good or bad advice or safe and unsafe people and, if we learn to interpret it, it will keep us protected and make our journey less painful.

We may question our Knowing, which is healthy, but we should always acknowledge its promptings. When we get strong urges, feelings, premonitions or notions, it is in our best interest to listen to them (this is when it helps to have a quiet mind). Their reasons may not be revealed for days, weeks, months or years, but if we ignore the Knowing's warnings, we often live to regret it.

Trait 2

Being in Public Places is Overwhelming

Shopping centers, stadiums, train stations or airports, where there are lots of people around, can fill the Empath with a mix of powerful emotions. Too often, these emotions, do not belong to them but are picked-up off others. It can take the Empath years to recognize that what they are feeling, when in public, is mostly coming from strangers.

In this heavily populated world, Empaths face many energetic challenges. If it is not harvesting strangers' emotions, it is having negative energies dumped on them, by those wanting to offload, or they are drained by the 'energy vampires'. It can become so problematic that being in public places becomes a source of anxiety.

Feeling and picking up other people's emotions is a trait many Empaths come to resent. Being Sensitive means we already experience enough overwhelming emotions of our own, without taking on the pain of others. The good news is, there are ways we can spend time in public without being taken down.

Self-protection is a must for those of a Sensitive nature and many Empaths are hard-wired into automatically doing this. However, sometimes life just gets in the way. It is too easy to get out of our protective routines or we may simply forget to take the necessary precautions before venturing out in public. We all need gentle reminders, from time to time, as to what we could be doing to protect ourselves and thus make life more enjoyable. And then there are times when we need to swap or change our usual 'protective techniques'. After all, life is about evolving and as we change and grow, so should our methods of protection.

For the Empath, blocking out all external emotions and energies is preferable but, sadly, it is not always that easy. For one thing, we are all connected and we cannot help but pick up other people's energy. The trick is in not allowing this energy to bring us down. We do this by not taking on, mentally, what we feel in others. Or, in other words, we don't acknowledge people's emotions (see next trait for more information).

When we repeatedly take on others' emotional energy, and claim it as our own, it may cause overwhelm or depression, especially when we are out-of-balance, and can lead to the Empath shunning all public places and even people!

If you are one who finds being in public areas, such as shopping malls and cinemas, unbearable, to the point of avoiding them at all costs, there are some techniques you could try that may help when you venture into people-packed-places. Here are some of my favorites:

My Top 11 Tools for Self-Protection

1. Salt: Most already know of the amazing healing properties of salt. It clears negative energies from the energy field and also helps us protect from absorbing them.

Here are some uses: Add it to you bath or use as a body scrub, before you go out or at the end of the day, invest in a salt lamp to help purify your home, and include salt in your diet (but always chose unrefined organic salt such as Himalayan rock salt).

2. Crystals: Crystals offer protection from many types of negative energies and help keep us in balance. They can also protect from electro-magnetic energy.

Choose the crystals you most resonate with. Carry them with you, wear them as jewelry, use them in meditations, sleep with them under your pillow or put them in your bath water.

3. Yoga: A short daily practice is a powerful protective tool for the Empath. Amongst many other amazing benefits, yoga helps balance and build our energetic shield, which in turn acts as an invisible force field, protecting us from taking on too much emotional energy. High intensity exercise is another great protective tool. Read more on the next trait.

4. Singing: Yes, this may seem bonkers but it works! Sound affects us on many levels energetically. Yogis have used sound for thousands of years (chanting/song) because they know the power of it. Singing raises our frequency, making negative energy bounce off. Try it when you feel an incoming energy storm and see how it changes your vibration.

5. Mirrored Energy Ball of Light: Every day, visualize yourself engulfed in a huge vibrant mirrored ball of protection. Do it before you plan to go out in public. Believe it is there and know it is protecting you from the unwanted energy of others.

6. Avoid Caffeine: Any kind of stimulant leaves the Empath wide open energetically. Too much caffeine in coffee may leave us unbalanced and vulnerable to other people's energy and is best avoided before going out or whilst in public places.

7. Breath-work: Certain yogic breathing techniques work wonders for raising our vibration. They help clear a muggy head and offer emotional energy protection.

A simple breathing exercise to try is: close the eyes and slowly inhale for 3-5 seconds, hold the breath for 3-5 seconds and then exhale for 3-5 seconds. Continue like this for a couple of minutes, or until you feel the engulfing calm of the breath.

8. Essential Oils: The power of essential oils has been known through the ages. As well as their amazing healing qualities, essential oils can help build a powerful energetic armor.

Essential oils work directly on the limbic system, activating the parasympathetic nervous system when we are stressed, which helps us to relax and shake off the excess energy we carry home.

As with crystals, chose the oil that resonates the most and make sure you enjoy their aroma. (My favorites are lavender, basil and frankincense.)

9. Close Your Eyes: (For obvious reasons, this should only be done when it is safe to do.) In noisy, highly charged places closing the eyes can protect from much of the wayward energies we would normally find seeping into our energy field.

Closing the eyes becomes extra effective when practicing a breathing technique at the same time. When we open them again the energy, noise or distraction, that had been previously pounding on us, seems to bounce off.

10. Balance the Chakras: This is the most important and effective of all these techniques. (And this also applies to men.)

Our hormones are directly linked to our chakras. If the chakras are out of sync the hormones will be too.

Unbalanced chakras affect both our physical and energetic bodies and when out of unison we cannot balance our own energy, never mind that of others.

11. Earthing: We so often overlook the power of the Earth to keep us grounded and protected, but it is one of the quickest and most effectual ways for self-protection.

Earthing is easy to do. As long as we have a skin on earth connection, by walking barefoot, standing, sitting or lying on the ground (grass, earth or beach) it reconnects us with the Earth's powerful energy.

Spending 5 to 10 minutes, connected to the Earth, is all that is need to stay grounded and protected.

Trait 3

Feeling Others' Emotions and Taking Them on as Their Own

Some Empaths feel emotions off those nearby and others feel them from those a short distance away, or both. The more adept Empath can tune into the emotions of individuals from a great distance away.

Feeling other people's emotions causes the Empath great distress.

To keep safe and sane, whilst walking this crazy planet, it is important to be able to discern between energies or emotions coming from our external environment and those that belong to us. This often proves to be a challenge for the Empath because it is too easy to mistake another person's pain and interpret it as our own.

It is relatively simple when entering a public place, such as a shopping mall, to recognize what we are taking on—on arriving, it can feel like we've walked into a wall of dense energy—but in the early stages of our Empath awakening we don't always understand this ability and it may cause stress and frustration.

Being flooded by sensory stimuli, from the thoughts and emotions of others, causes overwhelm, confusion and distress. But, because this ability is not always readily recognized, it is difficult to know how to prevent it from happening. A sudden barrage of emotions, belonging to another, can make us feel defenseless and weak.

Empaths become over-stimulated by other people's energy and emotions and is caused by being exposed to too much emotive stimuli. This stimulus is always felt worse by those who are out-of-balance or those who are unaware of their Empath abilities. Learning to recognize the many subtleties of external energy, and knowing how to unplug from them, is an essential component of Empath life.

Distinguishing between our emotions, and those of others, is essential if we want to find balance. This not only helps us cope with peoples' 'stuff' but assists in the understanding of our own emotional framework.

An Empath can be happy and relaxed one minute, enter a public place and within seconds feel any number of emotions that are coming from others.

As an Empath, we have experienced other people's emotions for most of our life but may only come to realize this in adult years. We sense these emotions in many ways. For example: We may have walked into a crowded room and noticed a heavy tension, even though everyone was smiling, or we may have felt deep pain in someone who is behaving in an upbeat, happy manner, or on entering a shopping mall, during the sales, detected an intense sense of anxiety as people panic buy and rush to get cut-price bargains. These are just a few ways of experiencing strangers' emotions or energy. There are countless more.

Recognizing Other People's Energy

Falsely identifying with another's emotional energy is easily done. When we pick up foreign emotions, we can get so wrapped up in the tornado of energy, that comes with them, that we do not question their origin. So how do we establish when something does not belong to us?

The best way to discern between our emotions and another's is to check if we had them before being in their company. If, when with people, we suddenly find ourself well up with certain emotions, that weren't there prior to being around them, they probably don't belong.

Depending on what we are experiencing in life will depend on how the emotions of others make us feel. If things have been steady, with no particular ups and downs, and we abruptly experience a torrent of negativity, when around people, we can easily identify it as belonging to another. However, if we are already in a troubled emotional place, and we pick up the low-level energy of another, it will simply connect with our own emotions and thoughts. Like attracts like. In these cases, defining emotions is difficult to do.

It is during the most trying of personal times that people's emotional energy causes the most pain. This is why it is important to learn to distinguish between their energy and our own.

As Empaths, we are hard-wired into picking up strong emotions in those around us. If we are in a dark place, we will attract more of this from others. For this and many other reasons we need to keep our vibration high and work to stay in balance.

The way we feel other people's energy is not just affected by what they are feeling. Our own emotions and moods play a part in how we interpret them. Moods are affected by our environment, diet, and lifestyle choices. These factors all influence how our hormones and brains work and thus affects the way we feel.

The impact of emotional energy is sensed around the solar-plexus (just above mid-stomach), which is the seat of emotions. The reactions caused by getting annoyed, offended or upset, builds from within. Whereas reactions triggered by other people's energy often seem like they are seeping in from the outside. When it doesn't belong to us, this energy is irritating and can stir up a series of strange but familiar responses such as: dread, anger, fear, prickliness, exasperation or overwhelm.

A quick way to determine the origin of uncomfortable emotions is to address them directly. When first sensing any negativity, that feels like it is coming from the outside say to yourself:

'I do not give permission for anyone's energy to infringe on mine. If this emotion belongs to another leave me now!'

Say it out loud or in your head. If the energy does not belong to us, it will loosen and we feel a distinct change in how the emotion feels. When we sense this shift or subsidence, it is important to distract ourself and get the mind away from the negative emotions.

Emotions turn into thoughts. Once our thoughts get wrapped up in other people's emotions there is no getting away from them.

Distraction is a formidable tool for taking one's focus off emotions. When not focusing on the powerful emotive reactions, coming from others, it is easier to stay detached from them.

You may have already discovered your own way of staying emotionally detached, but a good distraction tool is by making noise in your head: Singing, humming or chanting are a few ways to do this. Just like plugging in your ears and singing loudly blocks out external sounds, I've found this helps with outside energy too. And because we are focusing on the sound, it keeps us distracted.

Sensing Your Inner-Turmoil in Others

Just because we feel negative emotions in another, does not mean we do not have negativity in ourselves. When we are uneasy around certain people, it may be that we are picking up a trait we dislike about ourselves.

It is important for the Empath to uncover any hidden negative beliefs or emotions. Whilst we bury a side we loathe, we will never be happy or feel complete. Empaths bury undesirable traits because we know how destructive they are. But burying them does not lose them. They still show up and eventually cause damage. Often, many of the characteristics we conceal have been passed down the family line. But they can also be caused by imbalances within the body.

Hate, anger, jealousy and fear of rejection are the most common attributes people bury. Because they make us feel weak, we don't want to face them. But if we choose not to confront these emotional fears, we just end up picking them up in others by the law of attraction.

How Can We Protect Ourselves?

By building a strong energy field (aura or energetic body) it helps protect from picking up emotions. We can do this by strengthening the body and mind.

Being physically or mentally weak automatically weakens the energy field. Our energy field is our unseen shield which protects from invisible influences.

Suppressed emotions, poor diet, lack of exercise, a busy head, illness and emotional pain all contribute to weakening our energy body. This makes us more susceptible to picking up negative emotions belonging to others. By strengthening the body and mind it strengthens the energy field and keeps other people's 'emotional stuff' out. Exercise is a great way to do this. By doing regular 5 minute blasts of exercise (yoga or high intensity exercise), to the max, reaps huge benefits for repelling or processing negative emotional energy.

I once watched a documentary about how power plants protect themselves from the impact of solar flares (coronal mass ejections). It explained that at the time a solar flare is expected the power station cranks up the electricity in the grid to full. This leaves the energy of the flare with nowhere to go, it simply gets diffused though the grid. Doing this also prevents the solar flare from frying the entire circuit. This reminds me of what happens when we do vigorous exercise: When we work-out, we crank up our feel-good endorphins, this then raises our vibration and builds a stronger energy-shield. And, because our vibration is spinning much faster, other people's thoughts or emotions then either bounce off or get diffused into our energetic field.

Also, keeping a quiet mind helps us distinguish between the emotions we pick up off others and our own. This is another reason why meditation is so important for the Empath. A daily practice helps clear erratic thoughts, which then enables one to differentiate between the subtle variations in energy.

If you have never tried meditation before, begin with 5 minutes and gradually build up.

Here's a quick and easy technique to get you started:

Find a comfortable seated position, in a place you won't be disturbed, and close your eyes. Focusing on your breath start to count back from 300: 299, 298, 297, 296... If your mind starts to wander, or thoughts pop in your head, simply acknowledge them and then let them go. Don't engage them or it will put an end to your meditative practice.

By the time you have reached 1, you should find your mind has calmed. You can end the practice there or stay within the quiet space of your awareness for as long as you like.

Trait 4

Watching Violence, Cruelty or Tragedy on TV is Unbearable

The more attuned the Empath the worse the effect of visual violence and cruelty. Some may even find they have to stop watching TV and reading the newspapers altogether.

The more in tune you are as an Empath the more you see the world for what it is, and the more you are affected by the plights of others.

Reading newspapers becomes a challenge, especially the ones packed with lies, gossip and no real news, and the TV can become unbearable (In particular, any kind of program with gratuitous violence or cruelty).

Even watching reality-singing-shows is a heart-wrenching affair. Witnessing 'so-called' talent judges quash the dreams of young hopefuls, whose main ambition in life is to feel special, is excruciating to witness.

Humiliating people is not a form of entertainment for the Empath. It is an act of cruelty.

It seems inconceivable how many people love the early stages of talent shows, when many of the contestants are ridiculed for their lack of talent, only to stop watching when the show becomes about the 'real' competition. The initial stages of some TV talent shows turn the audience (at home and in the studio) into a crowd with mob mentality. Laughing and jeering at those whose only crime was to believe they had the capacity to make it in the world of showbiz.

The Empath's incredible sense of empathy tunes into the hurt of others, whether that is watching violence, pain or humiliation. An Empath is able to put themselves into the position of another and experience their anguish.

As well as the TV, another place Empaths pick up emotional discomfort is via social media.

Platforms such as Facebook or Twitter can fill the Empath with conflict. But it is not just the heart-wrenching stories that leave us in a spin and wanting to unplug.

Social media posts written by those showing-off, or disclosing a fantastic lifestyle, are often invisible proclamations of superiority. An Empath knows when posts are delivered to the world to make people feel inferior about their lives, even when they are disguised as an empowering message.

We have the ability to pick up the energies of all those who we are connected to on Facebook, or other social media outlets—both good and bad—which is often overwhelming. We sense intentions behind a post. We know a hidden sales-pitch when we see one, when someone is trying to make people jealous we feel it, and when individuals add posts with hidden agendas we know. And, it does not feel good.

Not watching violence, or cruelty, on TV and limiting social media time is important for the Empath's wellbeing.

If we spend too much time viewing, or engaging, negatively charged outlets we easily become wired, drained or depressed, and this happens whether we are in balance or not.

Trait 5

An Empath can Feel a Lie

If anyone, whether it be a friend, loved one or person in a position of power, is telling lies the Empath will feel it. They may not be aware of what the lie is but they feel the energy of an untruth as a strong sense of discomfort.

An issue many Empaths struggle with is deceit.

We come to learn that part of our journey is about learning to live with integrity and face our truths. But, in this current climate, it is becoming much harder to do.

Everywhere we look lies are spun like huge sticky webs of deceit, entangling people like helpless flies. But what makes this awkward to live with is the fact these lies go mostly ignored, even when they have been exposed.

Looking for answers and striving for the truth is an inbuilt trait of an Empath, which makes living in a world built on lies a difficult place to be.

A great deal of what we have been taught, or told, has been centered around falsehoods. So much so, it becomes difficult to discern between fact or fiction.

Empaths crave a life of authenticity, but find it difficult to achieve when we live in a society that breeds and feeds untruths.

Most of the political, educational or religious agendas, we have had rammed down our throats, are based on disinformation and are formed for the sake of profiteering and manipulation.

The powers that be have lied to make money, stay in power or manipulate us for devious gains. They persuaded us that the rules they make are put in place to keep us protected and safe. When in truth, we can see, they are just ways of control.

As Empaths, we know that much of what we have been told, by those in power, is based on partial truths, but the frustrating part is others don't.

For so long it has appeared that liars get rewarded and those who speak the truth get attacked. (But that is starting to change.)

Everywhere we look people are inhabiting a life of dishonesty, in complete acceptance, as if there was no other choice. But we always have a choice.

Lying is cheating and whilst we knowingly live, or go along with, a lie we will never find the peace we crave.

The fact is: lying and cheating are very easy to do but it is also cowardly. Honesty can be difficult to embody yet it is where true bravery is seen.

For some, it may seem as though we are being dishonest when we don't talk openly about our Empath traits. We could fear that if we express who we are we, what we feel, see and intuit, that we will be verbally criticized. But if we stay quiet about who we are it may seem like we are living a lie or leading a double life. This plants us firmly between a rock and a hard place.

We eventually come to realize that people fear what they do not understand. So not sharing our 'ways' is sometimes the safest policy. And besides, if no one asks about our 'Empath ways' we are not lying when we choose not to divulge our traits or what we know.

Priority should always be given to self-honesty (it is often harder to be honest with ourselves than it is with others).

I have discovered the most advantageous way to become liberated, as an Empath, is by being completely truthful with oneself first and foremost. This way of being uncovers the truths we have been denying, and lifts the blanket of shame we believed offered shelter, but instead imprisoned us.

Self-confrontation holds one of the keys to emotional freedom. That said, just because we uncover a truth, does not mean we have to share it with the world. Although it is true the more honest we are with others the freer we become, sharing has to be an organic process and not a forced one.

Sensitive people with always be sensitive, and criticism will often hurt, so we still need to protect ourselves from other people's harsh opinions and shortsightedness. As long as we accept our truths and live our own life with integrity, we are on the right path.

On our journey, we come to see the reason most lie (but not all) is because of their own insecurities and fears, and not as a way to hurt others. Knowing this can make the untruths easier to understand and tolerate. Inconsiderate behavior then becomes less painful to bare.

Times are changing and truths are finally being revealed, but it is often the case that things get worse before they get better.

If we live by example in our integrity, then we will see a change in the world... Be the change see the change!

32

Trait 6

Experiences Physical Symptoms of Another

Not only will an Empath feel other people's pain and emotions, and take them on as their own, they can also develop their ailments, somewhat like sympathy pains.

Although we frequently experience other people's ailments, it may take the Empath many years to recognize this trait.

We don't always know when we are picking up physical complaints because we don't always know what others are experiencing, physically.

It is very easy to feel an ache in the back or twitch in the eye, that comes and goes, and pass it off as one of those random tics or twinges, when we are in fact embodying another person's physicalities.

We can also manifest other peoples' ailments, like coughs, colds, eye infections, etc., without trying.

If we regularly exhibit the physical symptoms of those we spend time with, that tend to last, it is usually an indication of an impaired immune system. For this reason, (and others), it is of the utmost importance all Empaths keep a strong immune system to protect themselves.

An out-of-balance Empath need only briefly be in the presence of someone with the beginnings of a sniffle to receive a full-blown dose. Of which, the ensuing symptoms are often worse than those of the original carrier.

You have probably heard of the saying: 'like increases like?' Well, it works in all areas of life.

Generally, those of us who constantly experience negative emotions of others, or absorb their physical symptoms, will feel rubbish most of the time. When we feel rubbish, we want to eat rubbish! Processed, stodgy and sugary food is what I'm referring to. This type of food does not include much in the way of nutritional value.

So, we feel rubbish, eat rubbish, feel more rubbish and get no nutrients.

Nutrients are our safeguard against illness because they help keep the immune system resilient.

We already know nutrient devoid foods are no good for us, but when feeling low they are often what we crave. We also know that on our darker days, after being bombarded by the world and his wife's emotions, the family-sized block of sugary chocolate has a billion times more appeal than a delicious fresh salad. This is where supplements can help.

I came to realize, firsthand, the importance of supplements through unintentional trial and error.

In my haphazard approach to taking vitamins and minerals, over the years, I found that when taking supplements, I have far less immune-system-related illnesses than when not.

There is much controversy over the effectiveness of synthetic supplements and whether they actually work. Many health experts will argue that a healthy balanced diet is all we need for optimum nutritive levels. But even with the healthiest of diets do we really know how nutritiously balanced our food is?

It is well-known that our soil is no longer as rich in minerals as it once was. This affects the mineral content of the fruit and vegetables grown in it.

The ripe and brightly colored fruits we see on our supermarket shelves may have traveled half-way around the world, and are already months old, before they get into our kitchens. This means a much lower vitamin count than if delivered to the supermarkets within hours of being harvested.

Vitamin C and zinc are the go-to nutrients for building a healthy immune system. Taking supplements or eating foods rich in these nutrients is an easy way to protect oneself from developing the ailments of others. However, what works for one won't always work for another. So, when it comes to health, do the research and listen to the gut-sensations.

As an Empath, we constantly get that 'gut-sensation' telling us when something is off.

Listen to it in regards to supplements and diet.

If you have been feeling particularly run down or physically and mentally low, it is advisable to visit a nutrition expert before embarking on a supplementation plan.

There are lots of free information on the internet about supplements and nutritious foods, and it is well worth doing the research, especially if you are prone to accumulating other people's physical symptoms.

By changing the diet and increasing supplements the physical symptoms, picked up off others, have less effect, one's heath improves and it becomes easier to find balance in life.

Trait 7

Suffers Digestive Disorders and Lower Back Problems

The solar-plexus chakra is based in the center of the abdomen and is known as the seat of emotions. This is where Empaths, mostly, feel the incoming emotions of others and can contribute to a weakening of the area, leading to anything from stomach ulcers to IBS. Lower back problems may develop from being ungrounded or out-of-balance.

The one who has no knowledge of being an Empath will almost always be ungrounded. We find balance, and therefore become more protected from other people's energy, simply by learning to stay grounded. However, not all disorders in the digestive track or the lower back stem from being ungrounded.

Many Empaths suffer, physically, because of the stress-load we endure. The erratic emotions we shoulder, our own and those belonging to others, add to this stress-load. Any kind of stress leads to health problems and those who are Sensitive often have high, frenzied, tension levels.

The gut is the seat of our emotions and where we experience the impact of all we feel emotionally. Sensations such as stress, hurt, anger, fear, or other nervous tensions, leave a direct impression on the gut and a trail of damage. These nervous tensions activate the stress hormone cortisol (also known as the fat storing hormone. See more on trait 24).

Cortisol is produced by the adrenal cortex. Like adrenaline, it is emitted in times of stress. The more worry we endure the more cortisol is produced and the longer we remain in our anxious state.

Even from a young age, Empaths frequently experienced stomach aches, acid indigestion and bowel problems, as a direct result of emotional upset. Although everyone feels anger, fear and nervousness, in the belly, Empaths feel them more acutely. So much so it can weaken the area. This means we are vulnerable to experiencing disorders of the digestive tract.

It is important, when looking after our Sensitive health to take measures to heal, soothe and nourish our gut. Whether we think we have digestive problems or not.

The gut is integral to our entire nervous system. Those with poor gut health are known to suffer with conditions such as anxiety, panic disorder, stress, an overactive mind and erratic emotions.

When we heal the gut, we calm and heal the brain and body. The best way to achieve this is by cleaning up the diet, including dietary supplements, and by bringing calm into our life through practicing that which we find relaxing: e.g. meditation, a yoga practice or other creative outlets.

Lower back problems and digestive disorders are common in all Empaths. If you suffer with either and know they have not been caused by being ungrounded, taking on too much negative energy or from an underlying health condition, the next place to look is at the diet.

As already mentioned, there is lots of free information on the internet in regard to diet and supplementation, but if you want more detailed information, written specifically for the Empath, then my book 'The Eating Plan for Empaths and HSPs' covers diet and how it affects the Empath in great detail. It also explains some simple ways to transform your Empath life through the diet.

Trait 8

Always Looks Out for the Underdog:

Anyone who is suffering, in emotional pain or being bullied will draw the attention and compassion of an Empath.

It will cause hurt and distress for the Empath to watch someone emotionally suffering. Through our strong sense of empathy and compassion we relate to and understand those who are being bullied or singled out. But this trait can also work against us if we allow others to take advantage of our considerate ways.

People are very one-sided when it comes to hurting others. They know how it feels when someone hurts or lets them down, but are often incapable of seeing how their own actions cause damage.

Empaths tend to think before speaking, or taking actions, especially if our words or deeds could trigger pain for another. We consider how it might feel to be on the receiving end of disappointments and will empathically put ourselves in the shoes of another before we act.

The downside to this is we may give those who treat us badly too many chances and too much of our time, and put up with bad behavior because we do not want to cause a conflict or create ill-feeling.

Empaths frequently feel sorry for those we shouldn't. And for this reason, those who cause us emotional pain, through their selfish or narcissistic ways, often end up staying in our lives longer than they should... because we keep giving them chances.

Being in harmony with people is essential to our health and wellbeing. Toxic relationships cause untold damage.

If someone continuously causes us upset, or disappointment, it may be time to evaluate the relationship and perhaps release them for our life. Before we can really be of service to others, we have to find balance within, and that means taking care of our physical and mental needs, and stop exposing ourselves to anything which is toxic in the form of food, substances or people.

Most of us know at least one toxic person, who activate a host of extreme and undesirable emotional reactions within. These folks seem to spew venom when they talk. Their noxious vibrations are felt in any of the main chakras—but especially in the solar-plexus—in the form of an ache, pull or burning sensation.

It is normal for toxic people to talk negatively of everyone and everything, which can drain an Empath's life-force within a matter of minutes. Even after trying every trick in the book, for self-protection, it seems nothing will stop their offensive energy from seeping into our physical and energetic body.

Because toxic friends are often family members, or a lifelong buddy, we are naturally concerned about letting them go, not least because we don't want to hurt them. But if we tried helping them, by sharing what has helped us in dealing with the rigors of life, or if we changed ourselves, to be more of who they want us to be, and they are still not happy, there is not much more we can do. (Read more about toxic friends on trait 25).

Sadly, there will always be those who do not want to hear about any kind of self-help, no matter how in pain they are. Instead they expect us to listen as they offload their negative rants. We may have urged them to see their situation from different perspectives, hoping they may recognize only they hold the power to change their world... to no avail.

An Empath's ardent inclination to look out for the underdog often means we stick our necks out for those who eventually cause us pain, even if this pain is produced indirectly by their negative energy.

As difficult as it is, we must always remember to put the emotional health of self, first. If we knew a food or substance made us violently ill or caused depression, we would avoid it. The same should be applied to those who trigger emotional turmoil. It is one thing looking out for the underdog, and protecting those in need, but if they refuse to help themselves, and start to rely on us, we are not helping them or ourselves.

We have a responsibility to keep our bodies and mental wellbeing healthy. If anyone triggers our stress levels (all stress eventually leads to illness), it is our duty to either confront the said person or remove them from our life.

I am not talking about having our ego dented by another's random disrespect. We all have people who offend, hurt or make us angry, by their lack of understanding. We in turn, no doubt, do the same to others. But those who repetitively bring us down will eventually do immense emotional and physical damage.

Looking out for the underdog is a rare and admirable quality, but we still have to look after ourself. Allowing another to take advantage of a kind heart, or continuously cause physical or emotional pain, will bring a deficit to our personal power. This deficit then weakens our mind, body and spirit.

Trait 9

Friends & Strangers Offload Their Problems

An Empath can become a magnet for everyone else's problems. If they're not careful these problems end up as their own.

In their quest to help and serve, Empaths need to be wary of not becoming an emotional-dumping-ground for everyone else's issues.

People come to an Empath because we listen and hear what they have to say. As this is rare in today's society, it becomes like a drug to those who want to be heard. This is one of the main reasons some Empaths close themselves off to others because we can only take so much.

Empaths must serve their needs first and learn to say "no" to those wanting to offload or take their time. I am not saying don't lend an ear, or be there for those in need, but if they keep coming with the same 'victim-mentality-me-me-me' stories they are just stealing our time and energy, and this helps no one.

If anything, we need to help others to help themselves. If we do more than that we risk stripping away their opportunity for lessons and growth.

If someone does not want to hear the advice we offer, it is not our responsibility to force them to hear us. They have to make a change when they are ready to make it and it has to be an unforced process which feels right to them.

Empaths generally know who want to listen and those who don't.

When talking to one who doesn't want to hear us, even when they act interested in what we are saying, we normally feel an internal compression. It may feel like the torso is being squeezed and we experience a definite reluctance to talk. For example: whilst engaging a friend in conversation waves of heaviness, or boredom, wash over us the second we start to speak. This is a classic Empath signal. We are picking up their vibrational suggestions that they don't want to hear what we have to say. This isn't because we are boring them. It is because they are keen to resume talking about their 'stuff' and nothing else.

It will serve us well if we choose not to be offended by other people's one-sidedness or lack of interest. Most are oblivious to the needs or sensitivities of others. Life is challenging for everyone and there are few who have little, or no, conflict going on in their life. Unfortunately, not everyone is ready to hear what we know. Many Empaths become frustrated by this and feel they are not doing enough to assist.

It is difficult to see anyone suffering, whilst knowing the steps they could use to help themselves but not be able to pass it on. However, we eventually learn to take a step back.

When it comes to listening, we have to remember to keep our boundaries, of protection, and know our time limits. The last thing we need is to take on the woes of those offloading. And we should not feel guilty for excusing ourself from anyone, who is unburdening themselves, if their woes become too draining.

If we take on too much, it will deplete us. Once depleted, we are at risk of being filled with negativity and unpleasant emotions, or getting ill.

Trait 10

Often Endures Chronic Empath Fatigue

Empath fatigue (E.F.) is caused by too much social stimulation or picking up excessive amounts of emotional energy.

Empath fatigue can be one of the worst physical traits an Empath has to deal with. It often takes us out of action faster than anything. This type of fatigue is exhausting and is triggered by spending too much time around certain people or experiencing too much stimuli, especially when one is out-of-balance.

When struck down with a dose of Empath fatigue simply moving is hard work. The body feels like a lead weight—making any kind of work or exercise a mammoth task—and the brain feels mushy, as if it's made of thick pea soup.

We mostly experience Empath fatigue after being around negative or draining people, but any kind of emotional stimuli will contribute to it. This crushing exhaustion is caused by spending too much time in busy, peopled places, like shopping centers; working in a job that requires a lot of social interaction or by spending too long with a group of friends (to name a few). We all experience it at some point in our life and once we do, it tends to reoccur. The fatigue is mostly chronic in nature and debilitating.

What Causes Empath Fatigue?

In a word, people! Being exposed to too many people for too long will trigger a flare-up that can lasts for days after exposure. It is caused from giving and receiving too much in the way of energy. We may wrongly assume that only negative experiences cause Empath fatigue, but this is not the case, it is caused by too much stimuli, good or bad. The more out-of-balance we are, the worst its effects.

Not only is this chronic fatigue debilitating, it can make our moods plummet.

Every Empath will vary in their degree of fatigue, and how it affects them, but it is a real side-effect of being peopled.

I liken E.F. to food intolerances, as it acts in a similar way.

Food intolerances cause physical discomforts after eating certain foods.

Intolerances are not to be confused with a food allergy where one endures a life-threatening reaction within minutes of ingesting an offending food. With food intolerances, we may be able to eat a small amount of a certain food and experience no reaction. For example: we be intolerant to almonds, but if we eat three almonds we have no response. However, if we were to eat five almonds, we get a big reaction. This is similar to how Empath fatigue works, but instead of digesting too much of an aggravating food we process too much sensory stimuli.

We may not be aware of it at the time, but when we are in social environments, we experience many highs and lows, both emotionally and energetically: A friend may relay a story that acts as a trauma trigger or we might pick up emotions from a buddy who is depressed, yet pretending otherwise, or we could attract emotional energy from someone sitting at the next table who we have had no contact with. Any of the above, energetic interactions, could initiate a big dose of E.F.

The best way to prevent, or recover from, Empath fatigue is by knowing one's time limits—when in social situations—and sticking with them, avoiding negative people or energy vampires, and by finding balance within the mind, body and spirit.

Trait 11

Owns an Addictive Personality

Empaths become addicted to substances such as alcohol, drugs or food as a form of self-protection. In order to hide from, or block out, negative energy they overindulge on addictive substances not realizing they actually heighten Empath overwhelm.

Being highly reactive, Empaths respond more to drugs or drug-like foods than those not of a Sensitive nature. They taste the bitterness in lemons more than others, feel emotional and physical pain more, and are affected by drugs and alcohol worse than those who are not highly reactive.

As 'high reactives' we are acutely responsive to the many vibrations of energy. Everything is energy vibrating at different frequencies and that includes food, drugs or alcohol. The lower the vibration, the worst something is.

Empaths are overly affected by anything of a low vibration. Drugs, alcohol and certain foods have a low vibrational energy. They bring us down emotionally, physically and energetically (even though they may initially appear to do the opposite) and enhance negativity.

In a bid to counteract, or numb, negative emotional energy, we often overindulge in that which gives an instant pleasure hit. Because of this, we unwittingly become addicted to foods that behave like drugs in the body, such as wheat and sugar. Not realizing they act like opiates on the brain and are habit-forming. Once eaten, they may give a quick release of pleasure, in the form of an induced high, but the relief obtained is only temporary and comes with an almighty emotional hangover. After the 'pleasure effect' wears off the brain then craves more of these food-fixes to get back the pleasurable high.

The short-term pleasure that drugs (including alcohol), or drug-like foods, offer puts us on an unsettling emotional roller-coaster. We then need to have more of the addictive substances to quell any discomfort they initially caused. And if consumed regularly, they not only amplify all inner-fears, and unpleasant feelings, but create an unbalanced mental state.

Unfortunately, any kind of stimulant (alcohol, drugs, etc.) only serve in weakening the Empath, as they do any other human. Under the influence, it may appear external energies are being obstructed but, regrettably, this is not the case. They still seep in and still affect us.

Whilst imbibing alcohol, when in company, other people's emotions can show up within the Empath's psyche as aggression or an overly dominant ego. This is a reason many Empaths find their moods significantly alter when consuming alcohol. The day after consumption there will generally be a physical and emotional hangover to contend with too.

The Path of Pleasure or Pain

The strongest driving-force in life, for all humans, is the desire to feel pleasure and evade pain. Most go out of their way to avoid anything that creates emotional or physical discomfort, but are also strongly drawn to that which gives the greatest pleasure.

The most common form of pain, experienced on a daily basis, is emotional and is caused by how we perceive our world. Speculative worries of the future, fear of being judged, fear of failure, or fear of not being liked, all lead to emotional pain. As do embarrassment, mortification and the many feelings that go with the perception of failure. But by indulging destructive addictions, in our bid to escape pain, we actually enhance it.

Empaths gravitate towards emotional discomfort. Not by choice I might add, but by the law of attraction. Like attracts like. When we wear emotional pain, like a badge, (whether it is ours or not), we draw in more of it. Feeling the sorrows of others—which become our own if we're not careful—only adds to our load. When we are psychologically low, we are open to attract more low feelings.

The public may disguise their angsts and insecurities, behind pleasantries and smiles, but, as Empaths, we still draw in this unstable energy without trying. Spending time in the world can then become like crossing a minefield. And this is why many of us overindulge in addictive substances... to blot the pain.

Anything addictive has low vibrational energy and will further activate negative emotions.

For the reason that Empaths experience countless overwhelming emotions, it serves us to discontinue consuming addictive foods, and other substances, that heighten them.

If you feel ready to make the transition, into stimulant-free lifestyle, why not find a healthy addiction instead? There are enough to try: yoga, exercise or clean eating, to name a few. Or why not throw yourself into a new passion? As Empaths, we are hard-wired into seeking out fresh ideas, passions or pleasurable pastimes. When we take our focus from a bad addiction and move it to a good one, it acts as a clever distraction. We can then avoid the usual discomfort and resistance which comes when giving up harmful addictions.

Trait 12

Drawn to the Metaphysical and Healing Therapies

Empaths are natural healers. They are drawn to healing like a moth to a flame. But many end up turning away from it, after they've studied and qualified, because they take on too much from the one they are trying to heal.

Anything of a supernatural or metaphysical nature is of interest to the Empath and they don't surprise or get shocked easily. Even at the revelation of what some may consider as astonishing or unbelievable.

Because we have an inbuilt curiosity of healing and spiritual matters, and are often natural healers, we may think it is an area we should work in. I do not believe that this has to be the case. At least not for all Empaths. I myself qualified in many healing and holistic therapies but practice none. I trained in them because I believed I had a responsibility to get out into the world and help heal it. But, in doing so, I discovered I took on too much energy from those I worked on.

I had an incredible fascination and ability to perform healing techniques, but I did not enjoy the way I felt afterwards.

When I explained to others how practicing healing made me feel I got the usual, 'Oh you need to ground yourself.' or 'Close yourself down after.' I did both, but it did not help. I still felt awful and overwhelmed. I came to understand the reason was because I was not supposed to be working as a healer. It was not my purpose or my path.

I now know I was attracted to healing because it was vital for me to gain a deeper understanding of how energy, and healing energy, works.

If you too are drawn to healing, or helping others, but find you get overwhelmed when spending time around people, don't be discouraged. We don't always have to work on the frontlines to be of service. We can do important healing work in many weird and wonderful ways. Simply listening to another is therapeutic for the one being heard. However, if you know in your heart that you want an occupation as a healer, but worry about getting 'peopled', it is still a doable path for the Empath.

Before one should embark on a life as a healer, it is essential to find balance in the mind, body and spirit. If we are not physically strong, we will be energetically weak. And if we possess a leaky aura, we are not a good conduit for healing energy.

A weakened body and mind weakens our energetic body (aura). Low-level thoughts and emotions, unbalanced chakras, food intolerances, poor diet, drugs and alcohol all impair the body, and anything that debilitates the body damages our aura.

When the aura is damaged, it becomes leaky. This is bad news on many levels: it allows our energy out (causing fatigue and other imbalances), and admits other people's energy in, which then merges with our own.

So, before we attempt any type of healing work we should endeavor to heal the aura.

It is also important to have a suitable understanding of staying grounded and protected before practicing healing treatments.

Trait 13

Enjoys Being Creative

From performing, drawing or writing, an Empath will boast a strong creative streak and have a vivid imagination. Empaths need to participate in some sort of innovative outlet for their soul growth. Being creative allows for incredible self-development and freethinking, it literally frees the Empath heart.

We live in a world governed by laws, and we go through life being expected to follow rules, rules and more rules. When we are controlled, in such a way, it does not allow much room for creativity and freethought.

Being creative gives access to our childlike imagination and allows us to bring our aspirations into fruition. It is not only innovating but liberating!

Being innovative helps balance the brain, builds intuition, encourages us to think 'outside of the box' and see the world the way it really is.

Creativity also keeps our curiosity alive and is the perfect way to free the mind: unleashing all those hidden magical aspects of life that have been buried beneath a regime of rules and control.

Spending time creatively puts us on the path to finding our true Empath self and to finding a place where happiness blooms.

One of the greatest causes of unhappiness on this planet is people not knowing themselves or what direction they should be taking. And, because Empaths are a rare breed, this makes self-discovery even more of a challenge. When we express ourself creatively it aligns us to our truth. And the resourceful parts of the brain, that have remained dormant by a life governed by rules, are activated.

Any Empath who does not articulate herself creatively will feel trapped and uninspired and her natural inquisitive nature is suppressed.

Some Empaths may assume they don't possess an inventive imagination, but it is more likely they have yet to find a creative outlet that is a fit.

We don't have to be a master crafter or award-winning composer to indulge in creativity. Simply making a dance routine, writing a poem, arranging flowers or devising a menu, are forms of innovation. It is simply using the imagination to create. And we all have that ability.

When drawn to a craft or art, it will likely be a skill in which we will excel. Empaths are often good at anything we try our hand at as long as it is a role we enjoy.

Because we experience people in many ways, and unintentionally get inside the minds of others, Empaths make great actors and performers. We easily mimic behavior patterns and convey this in performance.

One matter which may hinder the Empath, from attempting any of the arts, is the fear of being judged. We might love the idea of being up on stage, writing a book, or singing in a talent show, but if a fear of judgment holds us back we miss out on the opportunity.

Empaths feel the energy of judgments even when they have not been spoken. Being judged or criticized can cause hurt and severely weaken those who are Sensitive. But the truth is, as an Empath, we should never let the fear of judgment prevent us from trying (I know, easier said than done). There will always be at least one person who judges, in a critical way, no matter how well we have done!

Those who judge have an issue with themselves and not with those they are judging. Too much of our short time here on Earth is wasted worrying what others think. Instead, we should ignore the judgers and get on with all the amazing artistic outlets life has to offer. They will judge us if we do or we don't.

Being Creative is our Time to Play

Drawing, painting, doodling, acting, clowning, writing, flower arranging, pottery, gardening, composing music, cooking, jewelry making, knitting and garment design are just some different ways of being creative. To truly create we need to make the rules, allow ourselves freedom to experiment and use our imaginations. Our creative-time should be classed as our playtime.

If you are not sure where you could express your creativity why not start with one of the many forms of exercise or dance? In the Western world, most turn to exercise for the benefits of weight-loss and a toned body. However, exercise and dance offers so much more: it can release pent-up emotions, remove impurities through sweat, enhances and uplifts moods, balances the left and right sides of the brain, energizes, and allows us to have fun and become inspired. It is also a starting place for the creative mind to expand.

Some may be stuck in a boring exercise routine they do out of necessity rather than enjoyment. If this is the case, find something you love. What did you love to do as a child? If you detested running, and were no good at it, chances are it will be the same now.

Creative workouts are incredibly grounding for the Empath. To exercise creatively: get the music cranked up and boogie like nobody's watching (which it's probably best if no one is). Dance, stretch and jump your cares away, lift weights, do squats and get sweating. All you need is 5 or 10 minutes, but I guarantee if you're doing something you love those 10 minutes easily turn into 20, 30 or 40...

Keeping fit, creatively, helps clear the energy field, it boosts confidence, eliminates stress (yours and others) and is a great stepping stone to open up other creative outlets.

If we do what we love and love what we do, we will be happy... Happiness is crucial to Empath success!

Trait 14

Love of Nature and Animals

Being outdoors, in Nature, is a must for the Empath, and they have a deep bond with the animal kingdom.

There is nothing more healing to the body, mind and spirit than being out in Nature. A stroll through a beautiful woodland, over a grassy meadow or near a natural-flowing stream, not only has an uplifting effect but is also grounding.

Grounding is an essential component for the Empath's wellbeing. It is not by chance we have an innate love of being outdoors. Spending time in Nature keeps us rooted and cleanses our auric field of stagnated energy. If left un-cleared, this energy creates imbalance within the body.

When in Nature, it is also a suitable time to get out of our head. We can do this by using a technique called mindfulness.

Mindfulness is the act of being meditatively observant whilst allowing the breath to keep us relaxed.

An effective way to practice mindfulness, when taking a stroll in Nature, is to focus on the breath whilst walking. Gently inhale for a count of three then exhale for three counts—this in itself will help calm the brain—then take your awareness to something outside the mind: look up at the trees and notice all you can about the bark, branches and leaves, see the different cloud formations in the sky or inspect the wild flowers growing within the foliage. By doing this, we externalize our awareness and bring balance to the mind and emotions.

If you work or live in a city, with no access to parkland, make sure you step out at weekends, away from cars and air pollution. Taking your dog (or a neighbor's) for a long, leisurely walk is not only good company, if one is walking alone, but is also great entertainment. Dogs love being in Nature and get up to all sorts of tricks whilst nosing through the undergrowth or bounding through the sand or shallow waters. It's hard not to appreciate their enthusiasm and endless joy for life.

Empaths love animals because they give off such a 'clean' healing energy. Dogs especially emit powerful loving vibes. It is difficult for the Empath not to be drawn to dogs, or other animals, and likewise for the animal not to be drawn to the Empath.

Being in Nature is the perfect place to unite with the world's wildlife and is a space where we can feel complete gratitude for being alive. The natural elements are the most powerfully healing tools for the Empaths—as they are for all humans—and the more time we spend outdoors (in the woods, forests, fields or by the sea) the stronger and happier we will be!

Trait 15

Need for Solitude

An Empath will go stir-crazy if they don't get time to retreat from the world. Time alone is an essential component of their wellbeing; this is even obvious in Empath children.

Having a quiet space to retreat to is the Empath's chance to recharge, clear unwanted energy—picked up from others—and take time to relax.

When around people, we not only absorb their energy but their thought-forms as well, and they do not have to be negative to be draining. Being alone allows us time to breathe through and release all that we take on.

Another bonus of alone time is having the chance to be our true authentic selves. Not having to put on a 'people-pleasing-show', or act like we are unaffected by the energy and ways of others, feels so good that we may resent having to leave our personal sanctuaries. When we have to wear a mask of compliance, or inhabit a reality that doesn't quite seem a fit, we may do so begrudgingly.

When overwhelmed, tired or emotionally drained, it feels right to withdraw and hide away in a place where no one can reach us.

As Empaths, we want to be grumpy if we feel grumpy; if we are aggrieved we want to lick our wounds in private and process the pain by ourself, and we need time alone to manage everything we pick up energetically. This is why staying out of sight, 'under our stone', becomes utterly delicious and addictive. It is here we get to live our truth whilst taking shelter from the rat race of life. And there is no shame in taking shelter when external conditions are bad.

I believe that if it feels right to cut off from society, at certain times in life, then it is right.

Spending time 'under our stone,' is our time for growth. When away from the noise of negativity and distraction, we get to face ourselves and uncover our deepest pain and fears. It is also during these periods when we hear the gentle voice of our inner-guidance steering us towards the path to heal, repair and evolve. So yes, time alone is imperative for the Empath.

Be sure to schedule down-time in your life, even if it is a half-hour soak in the bath (preferably with salt) or to take an extra-long shower. Make me-time a priority and don't feel guilty for taking it.

Trait 16

Gets Bored or Distracted Easily

To keep the Empath mind engaged, work, school and home life must be kept interesting; otherwise their time will be spent daydreaming or doodling their way through a tedious job, lecture or routine.

An Empath knows there is no point learning a subject unless it is beneficial to their journey. For them, it is senseless learning extensive math or algebra, for example, if there is no place for it in their future.

Although we may not have a clear mental vision of what the future holds, our inner-Knowing does. It guides and serves us well. If a topic will be of no use on our path, we find ourselves subconsciously disengaging. And if taught anything that does not feel like a truth, or if it bears no interest, we soon detach. That is not to say we won't consider new ideas or a difference in opinion. We are always eager to learn and discover new information, but it has to feel like an acceptable truth before we engage it.

Having an active and creative mind means we are easily distracted. We maintain good mental focus when occupied doing what we love—because our passions keep us engrossed—but when we are bored, our mind becomes restless and deviates attention from the task-in-hand to a subject of more interest.

Being creative and doing what we enjoy is one of the best ways to keep the Empath mind contented.

Sadly, in a world of rules and routine, we seldom get time to be creative. Creativity is essential for all Empaths.

When we create, from our passions or interests, it has an uplifting effect on our psyche and because we're engaging in something we love, it keeps our minds away from the dark thoughts and feelings picked up from others (or indeed our own if we are prone to melancholy).

Staying away from that which tires our mind and drains our spirit—which includes people, pastimes and work—is a vital ingredient for Empath joy.

One who is bored or disgruntled often finds their focus drawn to un-pleasantries, negative energy and situations, and this is the last place an Empath's attention needs to be.

Trait 17

Finds It Difficult to Do What They Do Not Enjoy

To be involved in a job, or pastime, they have little passion for is a form of punishment to the Empath. To force them into doing anything they dislike—through guilt or labeling them as idle—will only serve in making the Empath frustrated and unhappy. Because they avoid undertaking tasks they don't take pleasure in, many Empaths get branded as being lazy.

This trait goes hand-in-hand with the last and ties in with the Empath's desire to live an authentic life.

So much of our short lives can be wasted doing what others want, or expect, of us instead of following our heart's desires. Life passes by too quickly. If we are not careful we could squander half of it doing a job that holds no meaning. Missing opportunities to accomplish ambitions, whilst laboring purely for income, is something most people come to regret in later life. But this way of being will also, slowly but surely, bleed the Empath of joy and leave a deep, dark void within the soul.

Empaths are free-spirits who resent being bound by pointless or laborious routines. We want to do work that reflects our truth and passions, and we want nothing more than to be able to express ourselves authentically. Sadly, the world we live in can make this difficult to do.

Finding a job, we are happy with, does not always come easy for the Empath. We spend much of life discovering roles we don't enjoy rather than what we do. Living a lie, by pretending to enjoy a job we dislike, or sell a product we have no faith in, is nothing short of torture.

If as an Empath you feel stuck doing work that brings no joy, or if it is causing great unhappiness, perhaps it's time to tune into your intuition.

When we listen, our intuition continuously presents vocational options. They normally come as urges or ideas to try a certain skill. We don't always recognize the guiding voice of our intuition, especially if we have a busy mind, but it will always endeavor to grab our attention.

If a new idea involves stepping out of our comfort zone, we may not want to hear what the intuition has to say, but if it is a match to our soul-purpose it will keep guiding us its way.

One of the best ways to access our intuition is through self-query. By asking the right questions, it helps open the mind to our inner-Knowing. For example, if searching for the dream job, or just a new direction in life, we could ask ourself the following questions:

- What are my passions?
- What do I love to do?
- What do I believe in?
- What would I wake-up excited to do each day?
- What can I not live without doing?
- What engages me?
- What interest keeps coming back to me?
- If I could change the world for the better, how would I do it?
- What work would I happily do for free?

Get a pen and paper out and write down the answers, to the above questions, as fast as you can. Don't stop to punctuate, or check if the responses make sense, just jot down what comes to mind.

When we transcribe our ideas, as opposed to mulling them over, we gain greater access to our intuition. This technique gives more insightful and genuine answers. It also enables us reread and further question our answers.

Use the above questions, or make a list of your own, to determine your true, or ideal, path, or just to get some insight into a current life-situation.

Trait 18

Strives for the Truth

This trait becomes evident when the Empath awakens to their gift. Untruths carry a dense, negative vibe which is disempowering to the Empath.

Because we live in a world where lying is 'quietly acceptable', even by respected leaders and people in power, it may take a while for this trait to be fully accepted or recognized.

Honesty, or more importantly self-honesty, is one of the most precious gifts we can give ourselves.

Because there is so much pressure to fit into the one-size-fits-all standards of society it is easy to lose sight of our true-selves, and when this happens we lose sight of our true-path.

It may sometimes seem that being an Empath sets us apart from the populace or that our quiet, Sensitive ways are not readily accepted, but we should not live in fear of rejection.

We can create prisons out of our worries about what others think of us, as well as the fear that we'll be spurned if we don't fit in. This is when we are in danger of creating fake personas. If we constantly pretend to be someone we are not, it will not only lead to unhappiness but also open up a gigantic void within. It is one thing putting on a mask, for short periods, when out in public, to better fit in or avoid conflict, but if we convince ourselves the mask is really part of who we are we could be heading for trouble.

As an Empath, we come to recognize the power of self-authenticity the more we practice it. The truth sets us free. Pursuing our truth may prove to be difficult but, in doing so, we are both rewarding and liberating ourselves.

If you are struggling to find yourself, I guarantee one of the reasons is you are not facing your truth.

We have not really been shown how to live our truth. We were told as children not to lie but rarely shown by example.

As an Empath, it has always been clear to see when someone is fibbing or pretending to be something they are not.

Even from an early age, we understood that expressing ourself truthfully is not always accepted and most people only see and hear what they want to see and hear, nothing else. These contradictions caused confusion in childhood, which continued into adulthood, and made searching for our truth a challenging quest.

Most Empaths believe the reason they hide from the world is to stay away from 'the negative energy of others', which is certainly a powerful motive, but it is not the sole reason. When we stay away from people—spending as much time as we can in our private sanctuaries—it leaves us free to be our true authentic-self. Not having to pretend, or fit in, with the expectations of others is a gift in itself. Alone time, therefore, becomes something we crave. This all comes down to the, inbred, Empath trait of striving for truth. Even if we are not 100% honest with ourselves, or others, deep down we want to be.

The fact we know not everyone is ready to hear the truth often prevents us from being open with them. But it does not mean we cannot be truthful with ourself.

We have to respect other people's journeys. If they are not ready for the truth that is their prerogative. We don't need to spend our time trying to convince them of anything, but it should not deter us from seeking our own truth.

Finding and facing our truth is no easy feat. We have so many layers of both societal and self-induced deceptions, built up, that we can only try to peel them back one by one.

Realizing our truths is not an overnight process, for some it can take years, but one of the fastest routes to unveiling them is through quizzical journaling.

Questioning ourself on paper (just as the exercise from the last trait), whilst allowing oneself to be brutally honest, accesses our intuition like nothing else. By spending between five to thirty minutes, each day, journaling it is one of the best ways to uncover any suppressed insecurities.

The way to start quizzical journaling is to have a question in mind, put pen to paper, and write down whatever comes to our awareness.

If, for example, you are being subjected to strong internal emotions, that you don't understand, ask yourself why you have them, then see what surfaces. You will be surprised by how much is revealed.

If worried someone may read your most private and intimate thoughts, destroy them soon after writing. This type of journaling isn't used as a way to chronicle our past but to uncover to our buried truths. They are truths we may have hidden to please others, or to avoid pain, and once revealed and understood we do not necessarily need to read them over and over again.

We cannot be free when bound by lies. Truth brings freedom. When we face our truth, and start being honest with ourselves, magic happens. We see life in a new light, we experience real gratitude and gain understanding of our Empath ways, and, most importantly, the truth of life begins to unveil and the steps we need for transformation are revealed.

Trait 19

Always Looking for Answers

Seeking knowledge and looking for answers is all part of an Empath's journey. There is much to learn and uncover about life's mysteries and it is in the curious Empath's nature to seek out all they can.

To find answers, and pursue the meaning of life, is to evolve as a human and an Empath. Not only from the standpoint of acquiring knowledge but as a way to learn what weakens or strengthen us.

By gaining wisdom we discover what brings balance to our mind, body and spirit, which then enables us to become empowered.

The journey of an Empath takes an interesting route, inherently filled with questions. And, it would seem, the more questions we have answered the more we find to question and the bigger the 'picture of life' turns out to be. Even if we have a wealth of knowledge rattling around in our brains, the longer we walk this path the more evident it becomes how much there is to learn and how little we really know.

On our quest for answers (and the truth), we learn, and unlearn, many things. We discover that it's ok to be wrong, it's ok to make mistakes, and it doesn't matter what others think of who we are, and we come to understand it is ok to be rejected for not fitting in with expectations. As long as we strive to be the best we can be, without harm to others, and are true to self, the mistakes or fails we may make on our journey, while looking for our answers, are our learning curves.

I believe the innate curious nature of an Empath is an inbuilt gift that serves a much higher purpose than most could imagine. Even if, whilst walking this plane, we don't recognize the objective of this gift, our inner-driving-force will continuously propel us forward, allowing us to obtain countless new insights as we go.

The inner-pain and conflict, many of us experience, aids an agenda for our soul-growth. If we did not endure all that we do—experiencing other people's pain as well as our own—we would unlikely search out the reasons, look for cures and in turn find the answers.

Our pain pushes us forward. Although to some it may seem like a curse, feeling everything so powerfully is truly a gift. It keeps our momentum alive by thrusting us into situations that keeps us looking for answers.

All the awakened Empaths of the world were prompted into this life, of self-exploration and searching for answers, by the discomfort we felt inside. In our bid to numb, or heal, our inner-pain, we were catapulted onto a journey of self-discovery. One question led to another. More and more doors were opened (different for each of us), and the more we learnt the more we grew.

'The more we discover the more we evolve and the greater we become as humans.'

As Empaths, we eventually come to learn that we are each 'ambassadors of life' with our own assignments to achieve. We learn, we grow, we ease our pain and strive for balance. We then pass on to others what we have learnt.

In comprehending that the only thing we get take from this life is our knowledge and experiences, it helps us figure out why we are given so many emotional encounters to overcome and learn from.

Empath life truly is a journey of exceptional evolvement. So, keep seeking, trust your intuition—and the answers you receive—and the bigger picture shall be revealed.

Trait 20

Craves Adventure, Freedom and Travel

Being free-spirits at heart means the tied down, or boxed in, Empath will feel imprisoned and unhappy. Having a sense of freedom allows the Empath to rejuvenate, therefore vacations and travel become a vital part of life.

Feeling free is essential for the Empath. Being able to take off at a moment's notice is energetically liberating and can play a big part in their levels of happiness. The Empath needs to know those in their life will allow for this. Even if they choose not to take off, habitually touring and trekking, knowing they can keeps their spirits elevated and instills a sense of independence.

Empaths always need an exit plan, whether on the phone, visiting a friend, or on a night out. We have to know we are not trapped.

Feeling stuck or confined is imprisoning and, if at any point, we are made to feel this way we will go out of our way to avoid that situation in the future.

Being trapped, whether in a one-sided conversation, in a place we do not want to be or with people we do not want to be with, will make an Empath fret and ignite waves of discomfort. And it is common to feel anxious and panicky when in a situation, we cannot freely walk away from.

If in a relationship, where we are denied a sense of independence, resentments will form. Anyone who tries to control or take away our freedom is essentially clipping our wings. Nothing beneficial will come from this, only our despondency.

In a world of control, rules and clock-watching, retaining a sense of freedom and adventure can be as simple as having time to take a short break, and visit somewhere new, or spend a day in a place of interest.

Even if we don't go on many vacations, for whatever reason, knowing we can, if even for a weekend trip, will prevent us from feeling restricted or trapped.

Maintaining a sense of, childlike, adventure and regularly having a change of scenery keeps the Empath's spirit soaring. It is an easy means to staying revitalized and centered. Even spending a night camping, in a forest or field, is an excellent way to keep the sense of free-living alive.

The more time we allow ourselves to wander and roam, the greater sense of adventure we retain and the happier we stay.

Trait 21

Abhors Clutter

Clutter creates stagnant energy which makes the Empath mind lethargic and uninspired.

An overly cluttered house leads to an overly cluttered mind and energy field.

Clutter equates to stagnated energy and is extremely draining to the body and mind. Even clutter that the eye cannot see still has a debilitating effect on the psyche and creates a congested feeling within our energy.

If you dwell in a crowded house (and I don't mean with people) you may not realize how much it drains you, causing physical apathy and an uninspired mind.

In the home, the Empath often opts for an uncomplicated decor, without too much fuss (ornaments, etc.), not realizing it is for the simple reason that all objects hold energy.

Too much of the wrong type of energy is overwhelming and, because we feel the draining effects of clutter, we have an inbuilt loathing for it. That is not to say our homes, or workplaces, won't contain some sort of chaotic mess, but it will constantly be at the back of our mind to get it cleared.

Over the years, clutter can, unintentionally, build and we may find the home becomes filled with all sorts of bric-à-brac, which only serves in being energy depleting. If, or when, this happens it is time to declutter.

The first thing we should summon, when decluttering, is bravery. Fear always rears its ugly head when letting anything go. It whispers in our ear, telling us how much we need those unused items, and gives all the reasons not to dispose of them. An unpredictable economic climate, or money issues, also prompts fear into goading us to hoard. So, although it may sound silly to suggest bravery, before starting a house clearance, it's exactly what we require.

Holding onto clutter only serves in dragging us down. And, unless we let go of the old, we can't make space for the new. If we can look around any room in our home and count five articles that serve no purpose, it is time for a clear-out.

Hoarding is born from the fear of lack. When we 'clear the clutter' we face this fear and it then loses its control over us.

The best way to ascertain what objects, or items, are needed is to ask this simple question: How will this improve my life? If you can't come up with an answer, other than it won't, it's probably time to ditch the item or give it to charity.

When our homes are cluttered, there is no room for anything new to come into our lives. In making space, we send out a message that we are open to receive (but hopefully not to more clutter) and we are ready for the new to arrive.

Clearing the clutter is not just for our possessions, we can also have an internal-clutter-clearing session. Disposing of old, limiting beliefs, habits or thought patterns, is both liberating and rejuvenating. Granted, they're not as easy to be rid of as belongings, but probably ten times more beneficial.

Clutter Clearing Check List for the Internal and External

- Does this serve me today?
- Will this serve me in the foreseeable future?
- Can this serve anyone else?
- Why am I holding onto this?
- In keeping this, will it make me happy?

It is not by chance Empaths intuitively abhor clutter. Deep down we know that collecting clutter, or hoarding, serves no higher purpose; but letting go of it does. It is said we develop more, as a human, by what we give up as opposed to what we acquire. And that includes habits and bad behaviors, beliefs, programming and possessions.

Clear your clutter today and feel for yourself the empowerment and incredible release that comes with it.

Trait 22

Loves to Daydream and Over-think

An Empath can stare into space in a world of their own, for hours on end, and be blissfully contented. When their thoughts are happy the Empath's mind is an enchanting place to be. But when thoughts are negative, their daydreams darken, causing unpleasant emotions and low moods.

Empaths have wonderfully creative minds that manifest many magical moments. However, couple this with an overly sensitive nature, where one feels heightened emotions, and the creative mind can become an enemy to the Empath.

It isn't just having one's feelings hurt that causes an Empath's thoughts to darken, picking up residual or negative energy also lowers their tone. And because thoughts are addictive, especially when they are troublesome, they are difficult to shake off.

Having pessimistic deliberations is a normal human trait. Most brood on dark, menacing ideas whilst the more positive reflections go unnoticed. Sadly, because an Empath has a penchant for deep-thinking, our reflective browsing too easily becomes a painful distraction from life.

If our daydreams turn into disagreeable musings, incarcerating our own mind and preventing us from living happily, it is time to take action.

It takes only 17 seconds for a negative thought to fuse. If we are not mindful, a random, undesirable, musing could escalate into hours-worth of dark repetitive thoughts.

Destructive thinking creates inner-stress and affects both our emotions and physical health.

Thoughts and emotions are interlinked. Over-thinking creates emotions and emotions trigger thoughts.

When we are triggered into irrational thinking, it is difficult to know whether the emotion prompted the thought or vice versa. Either way, it is best to stop the process before it builds momentum... that means catching thoughts within the 17 second window.

If thoughts darken, whilst enjoying a delicious daydreaming moment, it is wise to snap yourself out of your contemplations before they have a chance to multiply.

Dark deliberations are distinctly magnetic, they draw in more of the same. We have to resist the urge to engage them (easier said than done, I know) and instead distract the mind and place focus elsewhere.

If you struggle to come up with ways to keep the mind distracted, from repetitive menacing thoughts, here are some easy techniques to use:

- Sing a song, out loud or in your head.
- Recite poetry or a limerick.
- Get a crossword, or other puzzle, out and set to work on it.
- Focus on your breathing and count. back each breath from three hundred or practice pranayama.

- Give yourself a complex equation to figure out or go through the alphabet backwards.
- Do some vigorous exercise, dance or do a full-body shake-down.
- Get creative and do something you love that requires your complete focus.

Trait 23

Finds Routine, Rules or Control Imprisoning:

Anything that takes away their freedom is debilitating to an Empath. Being dominated by monotonous routine will poison their spirit and weaken their power.

Unnecessary routine and rules take away life's spontaneity and prevents freedom of spirit.

As Empaths, we did not come here to be imprisoned or controlled. We came to learn, evolve, live freely and authentically, discover our truths and make our mark. Sadly, many of us have not been able to live this way because of a control system that promotes limiting beliefs and offers a restricted existence by the way of senseless rules and grueling routine.

Having a doctrinarian life, mapped-out from womb to tomb, does not instill the sense of sovereignty we yearn for. Freewill is supposed to be a birthright, bestowed upon us all. But, in this age, it often seems more like a monetary gain than the gift it should be.

Being so easily, yet unintentionally, swayed by external thoughts, programming and the energy of others, we frequently imprison ourselves within a framework of emotional pain. And thus become trapped in a life that seems a million miles away from the one we want.

Before we can acquire the, authentic, life we crave—free from unreasonable constraints and draconian rules—we have to unplug from the fearmongering control system, we were born into, and stop allowing limiting, fearful beliefs to be the controlling voice within our head. This will go a long way to quelling the many fear-based emotions we suffer. These emotions are designed to keep the populace distracted, divided and controlled, but for the Empath they are also utterly soul-destroying.

It is not just the thoughts and beliefs, we indulge, that create our realities, our feelings play a huge part. We may not have consciously chosen the type of life we live but our energetic vibration did, through the law of attraction.

We attract what we think and feel. As mentioned in the last trait: our thoughts control our emotions and vice versa. This affects how we feel and vibrate.

If we are down or experience angry or other low-level moods, this is the type of energy we attract. The crazy thing is, these emotions may not even have belonged to us in the first place. Instead we picked them up from those we spend time with.

If we feel negativity—whether it belongs to us or not—we still vibrate this energy out and thus draw it back.

Feeling governed, emotionally, by that which we are not in control of, nor did we choose, causes frustration and resentment within the Empath. And not being able to 'switch off' these emotions is disempowering.

We need to remind ourselves that we are each the creator of our reality and we have the power to make the changes we want.

We get to decide whether we face triumph or defeat over what we feel. We choose our beliefs and our thoughts. And we can choose to feed the emotions (picked up from others or our own) more fuel or starve them completely (disengage them).

Recognizing that we truly have the power puts us back in control. This alone is transformative.

When we really get to know ourselves, find balance—of mind, body and spirit—and choose to live an empowered life, magnificent changes happen. We then start living by our own truth, rules and routine.

Although an Empath may dislike the idea of routine, it can actually be incredibly beneficial.

For example: having a daily practice of exercise, meditation and journaling (Exercise keeps the body and energy field strong, meditation keeps the mind quiet and clear, and journaling is a place to offload.) not only creates strength and balance, within the body and mind, but helps keep emotions in check too. Couple that with eating the right diet and we are already more than half-way to self-empowerment.

When we find our own routines and life-guidelines, that work for us individually, we become uplifted by them without feeling trapped or imprisoned.

Trait 24

Prone to Carry Weight Without Overeating

Excess belly, and body, fat can be caused by enduring overwhelming emotions. The hormonal reactions produced, from being hyper-sensitive to the energy of others, may promote fat storage within the Empath.

A protruding belly, as seen on many Sensitive folk, is often caused by an over-production of the hormone cortisol. Also known as the fat-storing hormone, cortisol is activated by the fight-or-flight response.

The fight-or-flight response—a protective reaction—is the body's way of giving us extra strength when in dangerous situations. Activated when we feel fear or stressful emotions, the process is designed, by Nature, to elevate certain hormones, giving us energy to run away from danger or stay and fight.

Two of the hormones released into the body, through the fight-or-flight response, are adrenalin and cortisol. These hormones, which are essential for increased body motion, increase heart-rate, respiration and glucose levels. When a stressful situation has passed, hormone levels and blood sugars should return to normal. However, when these hormones are constantly activated (by stress or fear) and not used (by running away or fighting), the blood glucose levels significantly increase. If there is too much glucose in the bloodstream, it becomes life-threatening, so the body removes the glucose from the blood and, with nowhere else to store it safely, it turns the glucose into fat. Which is often stored on the belly.

Empaths don't get away from stressful emotions easily. Not only do we have to deal with our own day-to-day stresses, but that of others too. We pick up emotions when in shopping centers, or other public places. Even residual energy can trigger a stress reaction. Depending how out-of-balance we are, some of these responses last for hours or anything up to a week. This means our fat-storing hormones, triggered by the fight-or-flight response, stay activated.

What Can we do About It?

1. Avoid known triggers: One of the biggest triggers being people. To protect ourself, we may need to stay away from those who activate negative emotions; at least until we have found such balance that we can be in their presence without being affected.

Those who act like trauma triggers, and bring nothing but stress and emotional pain, will eventually bring disease too.

2. Calm the mind and restrain unruly thoughts: By developing a regular meditation practice, it will help keep the mind calm and the emotions quiet. This will help prevent unnecessary cortisol activation.

3. Avoid stimulants: Caffeine is known to stimulate cortisol production. Empaths react to coffee and other stimulants more than most. Take note at which point you get a physical response—too much caffeine causes shakiness, pounding heart, flushing, faster-breathing and an aching chest—and don't consume enough to activate those reactions. Avoiding coffee altogether is sometimes the best option.

4. Exercise daily: Exercise is perfect for preventing excess belly/body fat. It helps use up surplus glucose, adrenalin and cortisol, in the bloodstream, and works as an all-round elixir for Empath wellbeing.

5. Control glucose levels through diet: The emotions picked up off others can cause excess glucose to be being dumped into our bloodstream. Low-carb eating drastically reduces glucose levels in the blood and prevents excess belly fat.

Because an Empath is vulnerable to having blood-sugar spikes and overly stressed adrenals, we cannot risk eating foods that worsen these effects. In my book: The Eating Plan for Empaths & HSPs, I explain the importance of diet to the Empath and how by making some small changes it can be transformative to life as well as to the midriff!

Trait 25

Excellent Listener:

Empaths love to listen. They know that by listening to another, without judgment and without offering their own opinion, is healing for the one being heard.

Empaths are born listeners. They often find people making a beeline for them, whether they know them or not, to offload their troubles.

In this fast-paced world, people rarely listen. Most are too busy thinking about their own narratives, or what they want to say next, to hear the story of others. This makes for many one-sided conversations. As Empaths, we listen and understand on many levels. We also care about what is being said.

There are sometimes downsides to being a great listener though. People may take advantage of our attentiveness, even good friends.

It is easy for people to become dependent on the generous listening nature of an Empath. For this reason, it is important to form good 'listening boundaries' (even with close friends and family), otherwise we take on too much.

Friends' energy, and how it affects the Empath, will change along with their age and life circumstances. If down or depressed, a friend may unintentionally take the Empath down with them. In these cases, the Empath has to unplug, emotionally. One can still listen and be there for the friend but in a more detached way.

When spending time with a troubled friend, or family member, we have to remain vigilante of any unwanted energy withdrawals. We all know people who are drainers, otherwise known as the 'energy vampires', but when a friend, who isn't normally a drainer, is experiencing a tough time their energy-sucking tentacles may seek out an instant uplift from anywhere, or anyone, they can. When we listen, and give another our complete focus, it could leave us energetically open and more prone to being drained.

So, to avoid becoming a friend's 'energy-replacement-meal', watch for any drain and where it is coming from. It will normally be from one of four of the main chakras: sacral (below the belly), solar-plexus (mid-belly), heart (heart-area) or throat (front of throat) and it can be felt by a pull or ache in that area. Wherever you feel it, cover the area immediately with your hands or arms. (It is not by chance we cross our arms over our stomach or chest in certain social situations; we are subconsciously stopping an unwanted energy-drain).

Being in harmony with the people in our life is essential to our health and wellbeing. We always want to help but we need to be wary of anyone taking too much, energetically, especially when it comes to offloading their troubles. Being there for others is a choice and not an obligation and it is our choice to whom we listen. Sadly, some friends, or family members, could cause the Empath more harm than good. Especially if, instead of making changes to their life, they expect us to be their emotional dumping ground.

Before we can really help, or be of service to anyone, we have to find balance within. That means taking care of our physical and mental needs and stop exposing ourselves to toxic energy, in the form of food, substances and people.

As already discussed, most Empaths will have at least one toxic person in their life, at any one time, and they are those who trigger harmful emotions or low moods. That is not to say toxic people are necessarily bad or evil, they just act like a poison to an Empath.

Here are some of the sensations you may experience when with people who have toxic energy:

- **Anger or feelings of bitterness**: This may last for the duration of time spent in their presence and up to 10 days after.
- **Fatigue**: Struggling to keep the eyes open, especially if they are venting.
- Being out of sorts: From being spaced out to feeling nauseous, a range of strange feelings can be experienced.
- **Negative talk**: Finding yourself talking negatively of others, even though it is not a typical trait. As Empaths, we easily mirror and morph into the people we spend time around

and end up joining in the rants of an overly toxic person.
- **Apathy**: Losing all previous zest and optimism.

Because friends, with toxic energy, are often family members, or lifelong friends, we may have a natural fear of letting them go. As Empaths, we don't want to cause anguish to others and, for this reason, we keep in our lives those who trigger emotional pain and frustration.

As already pointed out, we must remember to put our emotional health first. If we knew a food made us ill or caused deep depression, we would avoid it. The same courtesy should be applied to those who trigger inner-turmoil.

We have a responsibility to keep our body and mental wellbeing healthy. If another continuously causes inner-pain (all stresses eventually lead to illness), it is our duty to either confront the said person, about their behavior, or try to spend as little time in their presence as possible (obviously, I am not talking about one's children here).

Empaths project what they feel out onto others. We are each responsible for the energy we put into the world in the form of words, emotions and thoughts. If being in another's presence, or listening to them, is causing us to emit negative vibrations, it is our duty to stop being in said person's company, until the time when we know they no longer affect us.

Trait 26

Intolerance to Narcissism

Although kind and often tolerant of others, Empaths do not like to be around overly egotistical people, who put themselves first and refuse to consider anyone else's feelings or points of view.

Empaths often find themselves on the radar of those with a narcissistic nature. Where you find an Empath, you will find a narcissist nearby. There are many reasons for this. I believe one being Nature's way of creating balance. In the Empath, there is too much empathy and in the narcissist, too little. To create balance, Nature brings the two together.

Those with strengths in a certain area will often be paired with those who have weakness. We are then supposed to work together to find equilibrium. But, the problem we face is we haven't been shown how to do this. We were all thrown in at the deep end and left to figure it out for ourselves.

Instead of trying to rationalize, or understand, the reasons behind people's behavior, society teaches the populace to attack those who hurt us, or those who are deemed to be a threat. This way of being just puts people at loggerheads.

It is an inbuilt trait of an Empath to see life from all perspectives and to empathize with others. We often stay quiet about issues, or put up with bad behavior, in order to be the peacekeeper. But if taken advantage of we eventually snap. If someone repeatedly behaves in a cruel or selfish manner, the Empath will react. And if this involves a run-in with a narcissist it never normally ends well.

There is generally a no win situation when going up against a narcissist. They lie, cheat, see everything only from their perspective and then lie some more. The only way to win is to not get involved and walk away. Empaths often learn this the hard way after being burnt or watching others get burnt.

The dynamics of a narcissist and an Empath can prove to be a unique contradiction. They may have a natural aversion and an equal attraction. Some will say they are two sides of the same coin. I would certainly agree that an Empath and narcissist have heightened levels of sensitivity but it is expressed in opposite ways.

The Empath's sensitive side causes them to feel strong emotional pain and they get hurt easily. But it also contributes to their consideration, fierce loyalty and their abundance of empathy for others.

The narcissist's sensitivities also contribute to their emotional pain and getting offended. But, in most cases, their pain has made them bitter, resentful and vengeful. They have no empathy and when they have been offended it is often caused by a wounded ego as opposed to a pained soul (as in the Empath's case).

Trait 27

The Ability to Feel the Days of the Week

An Empath will get the 'Friday Feeling' if they work Fridays or not. They pick up on how the collective are feeling and share the excitement of others.

To the Empath, the first couple of days of a long bank holiday weekend (Easter for example) can feel like the world is smiling, calm and relaxed. Sunday and Monday evenings, of a working week, have a heavy vibe.

Those who work a 9 to 5, Monday to Friday, job could easily put the excitement of the 'Friday Feeling' down to looking forward to two days off at the weekend. On a Sunday, the sense of dread felt may be attributed to going back into work, especially if not overly keen on a job. However, as an Empath, if we have any extended time off, we soon realize we still experience the same workday sensations without going to a place of work.

Because the Empath picks up on vibrational energy emitted by others, we experience what the collective are enduring. If many people are having similar work-related moods we tune into the collective mindset and often claim it as our own.

The fact that eighty-percent of the workforce do not enjoy their jobs, and dread going back to work after the weekend, means the start of a working week can feel miserable. But as the week passes, and by the time Thursday comes around, the energy is lighter and happier. By Friday afternoon, there is that definite 'holiday feeling' in the air.

Experiencing the energy of workday vibrations may seem an unusual aspect of being an Empath, but it is simply another way we experience the collective's moods. It also goes to show just how powerful human feelings are.

Trait 28

Will Not Choose to Buy Antiques, Vintage or Second-Hand

Anything that's been pre-owned carries the energy of the previous owner, this creates a cluttered energy within an item.

Many people wrongly assume the reason trait 28 is on the list of Empath traits is because antiques hold negative energy, this is not the reason.

It is not unusual for antiques to be revered for their beauty and historical value. They are highly prized possessions. Even those not of a Sensitive nature will love to feel the energy and sense the history behind an antique. However, for some Empaths being around antiques, or anything pre-owned, can make us overwhelmed.

The reason for these feelings of discomfort is because anything pre-owned carries an imprint of the previous owner in the way of residual energy.

To some, this residual energy feels crowded or cluttered and, as many Empaths abhor clutter and crowding, we may have a natural aversion, even repulsion, to a second-hand item without knowing why.

Clutter equates to stagnated energy and is extremely draining to the body and mind.

Even clutter that the eye cannot see, held within an item or object, still has a debilitating effect with its 'clogged' vibration. This can lead to depleted momentum, feelings of sluggishness, apathy and an uninspired mind.

'Too much residual energy can lead to a cluttered mind and energy field!'

As with anything in life, there are always exceptions. There are some Empaths who love being around antiques and previously owned items; especially those who have the gift of psychometry.

Psychometry is a psychic gift which enables one to hold an object, such as a ring, and psychically receive detailed information about its past. Some Empaths are naturally gifted at psychometry but it is also a gift one can develop through practice.

Trait 29

Senses the Energy of Food

An Empath not only experiences the energy of the surrounding people, and their environment, they also sense the energy of what they consume.

Some Empaths give up meat or poultry, even though they like the taste, for the reason that when they eat it, they feel the vibrations of the animal (more so if the animal suffered).

Imprints of stress and pain, endured by the animal, is stored within its meat, which can be felt by an Empath.

Those who experience depression, after eating red meat, don't initially make the connection that it is triggered by the animal's suffering. However, the more aware an Empath becomes the more obvious it is.

The diet of any human is important but, for the Empath, eating compatible foods is vital for their physical and emotional health.

All Empaths are highly reactive to what goes in their body, via the mouth. The energy of food plays a huge part in how we show up in the world.

The wrong diet heightens the more negative aspects of being an Empath and subdues the more positive.

It can take the Empath many years to recognize that being Sensitive means we are susceptible to all forms of energy. Our diet can determine not only our levels of happiness but how we interpret the vibrations of people.

Even the way our food is cooked has an impact on an Empath.

Food prepared in an angry or unhappy environment, like a kitchen where there are many miserable staff, carries that low-level energy and thus affects how we feel.

To stay balanced in the mind, body and spirit, Empaths benefit from consuming a clean nutritious diet (when I say clean I mean without chemicals, stimulants and foods which are energetically compatible).

Eating home-cooked fare, where our meals are prepared with love, foods that are organic, without pesticides, and nutrient dense go a long way to keeping us emotionally stable and energetically strong.

Trait 30

Can Appear Moody, Shy, Aloof or Disconnected

Depending on how an Empath is feeling will depend on what face they show the world. They are prone to mood swings and, if they've taken on too much, may appear quiet and unsociable.

When under pressure or overwhelmed, Empaths often feel like scuttling under a stone, wanting nothing more than to hide from the world whilst we recharge. We detest having to pretend to be happy when we're sad or overcome by energy belonging to others, but we also don't want to offend anyone by our detachment.

There will be times when we appear quiet, aloof or unresponsive. It is this detached way of being that confuses others and is often mistaken for standoffish behavior. People may then wrongly assume we believe we are snobby or above them. But this couldn't be further from the truth.

When an Empath acts in an aloof or distant manner, it is often because we are overwhelmed. When on overload, after taking on too much stimuli from our surroundings, and in serious need of recharging, we want nothing more than to be invisible to others. The last thing we can deal with is polite conversation or someone who offloads their troubles on us. And it is at these times when we appear most detached. We shut down as a form of self-protection. But often find our still and self-reflecting ways are misinterpreted as disrespect.

It is never our intention to make others feel we are being offhand or superior, we really aren't, but our aloof ways are often interpreted that way. Sometimes we just need to retreat, even if it is into our own shell.

The fact that most people don't come close to experiencing what an Empath feels, means it is difficult for them to understand why we act the way we do. Sadly, the more insecure someone is, the more they will be offended by our, sporadic, reticent behavior. And if they believe we are acting cold or 'strange' towards them, they may reject or even verbally attack us.

It usually takes a while for our distant ways, or need for alone-time, not to be taken personally. We can spend too much time worrying about how our ways affect others instead of finding approaches to find balance within ourself.

When we come to recognize the triggers, that cause the many Empath highs and lows, life becomes more stable and happier. But no matter how balanced and in control we are, there will always be times when we need to retreat from the world, and we should give ourselves permission to do so...

~

So, there you have it 30 *'Traits of an Empath Uncovered'*.

I hope this book has offered you a better appreciation of your traits and how they impact your life.

If you struggle to express who you are, as an Empath, you could always hand this book to friends or family members to read.

It may help them gain a greater understanding of Empath ways and thus a greater understanding of you.

Other Books for Empaths
by Diane Kathrine

The Eating Plan for Empaths & HSPs – *Change Your Diet Change Your Life!*

7 Secrets of the Sensitive – *Harness the Empath's Hidden Power!*

Empath Power – *Grounding Healing and Protection for Life!*

The Empath Awakening – *Navigating Life in the Sensitive Lane*

Diane's Blog
www.theknowing1.wordpress.com

Printed in Great Britain
by Amazon